# Mice & Rats

K.W. Smith

S0-AWO-613

John Bartholomew & Son Limited
Edinburgh and London

*First published in Great Britain* 1976 *by*
JOHN BARTHOLOMEW & SON LIMITED
12 Duncan Street, Edinburgh EH9 1TA
And at 216 High Street, Bromley BR1 1PW

ISBN 0 7028 1072 X

1st edition

Designed and illustrated by Allard Design Group Limited
Printed in Great Britain by W. S. Cowell Limited, Ipswich, Suffolk

# Contents

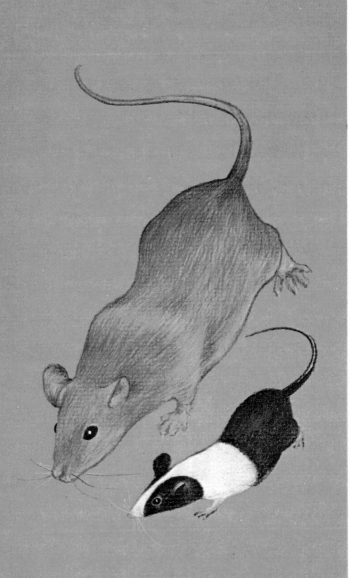

# Introduction

Undoubtedly the lesser rodents have now become the most popular of all small mammalian pets, not only due to restrictions of space in the average modern home but also in their own right: they are friendly, economical, and require the minimum of management. Fancy Mice have been kept as pets for so many years that they have become a standard attraction at agricultural shows in many parts of the world.

Yet prejudice still exists. All too many mouse owners know that immediate reaction from the unconverted masses; the look of horror from the false preconception that all mice are pests and that they create smells. On the contrary, although the Fancy Mouse is descended from the common wild House Mouse, *Mus musculus*, the pet of today is available in any one of a variety of colours, many of them aesthetically beautiful, and if looked after properly is guilty of no unpleasant odours at all.

Furthermore, a mouse in the house can teach children the responsibility of caring for it; a pair of mice can teach the basic facts of life, and may lead in later years to a deeper interest in genetics – or at least to an interest in competition showing of mice as a serious hobby.

If prejudice still exists towards the pet mouse, the pet rat, a close cousin, is prone to even stronger castigation from the uninitiated. But the rat is a very intelligent animal (is it not used in laboratories in experiments concerned with learning potential?) and its poor reputation is quite undeserved. Fortunately more and more people are coming to realise that pet rats are really very clean and make fascinating companions.

**Ancestors**

The Common Brown (or Norway) Rat, *Rattus norvegicus*: This species of wild rat, from which our Fancy Rat is descended, has been a constant companion of man for several thousand years. Its origins lie in Central Asia – despite its misleading alternative name – from which it spread to other parts of the world via the holds of ships. Although it originated in desert areas, *Rattus norvegicus*, like many of its fellow species, has adapted itself to almost every climate and environment, and can be found throughout the world.

The name of Norway Rat was given after reports showed that the animal reached the shores of Britain and America via Norway; the name has stayed with the animal ever since.

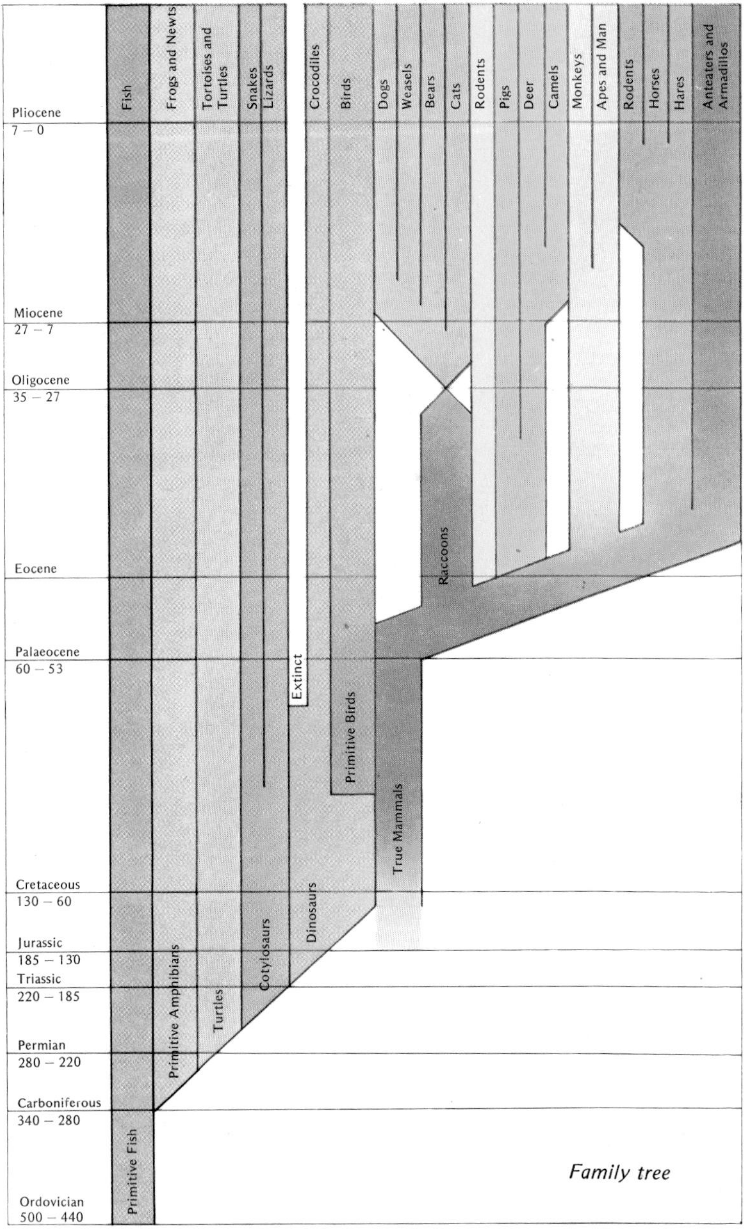
Pliocene
7 – 0
Miocene
27 – 7
Oligocene
35 – 27
Eocene
Palaeocene
60 – 53
Cretaceous
130 – 60
Jurassic
185 – 130
Triassic
220 – 185
Permian
280 – 220
Carboniferous
340 – 280
Ordovician
500 – 440
Fish
Frogs and Newts
Tortoises and Turtles
Snakes
Lizards
Crocodiles
Birds
Dogs
Weasels
Bears
Cats
Rodents
Pigs
Deer
Camels
Monkeys
Apes and Man
Rodents
Horses
Hares
Anteaters and Armadillos
Raccoons
Extinct
Primitive Birds
True Mammals
Dinosaurs
Cotylosaurs
Turtles
Primitive Amphibians
Primitive Fish
*Family tree*

The Brown Rat is somewhat larger than our Fancy Rat of today, growing to a body length of 10in – 12in with a tail a further 10in long, although specimens larger than this have been recorded. The rather dull coat is brownish-grey on the upper parts, shading to a light grey on the underside. Although wild-born members of the species can be tamed, this is not recommended : some of them can become very aggressive and are able to inflict serious wounds with their long incisor teeth if they feel threatened.

The Brown Rat is very adaptable and thrives wherever there is any form of food, whether it be in a grain store or a rubbish dump ; because of these habitats it can become an agent for the transmission of disease through the parasites it carries, though it must be stressed that it was the Black Rat which was responsible for distributing bubonic plague during the Middle Ages. Although the animal itself is never the carrier, it is this stigma that has rubbed off onto our Fancy Rat which has to prove, time and time again, that it is not like its wild ancestors and must be judged in its proper context.

The common or wild House Mouse, *Mus musculus* : Like its relation, *Rattus*, the Fancy Mouse has inherited a poor reputation. Though it is very destructive to crops and food stores, the mouse is potentially far less dangerous and does not present any real threat to human health ; perhaps because of this the Fancy Mouse is more readily accepted than the Fancy Rat.

*Mus* also originated in Asia and spread throughout the world with the help of man, again proving itself to be very hardy and adaptable. The wild House Mouse is much the same size as the Fancy Mouse, if anything a little smaller, measuring about 3in in body with a tail of equal length. The fur colour varies slightly according to distribution, but is in general a darkish grey on the upper parts, shading to an almost white underside, though light-grey specimens have been reported.

The wild House Mouse can be tamed if caught young enough, but this is scarcely to be recommended.

## Variations on the theme

The breeder or fancier has a number of types of mouse from which to choose, and although this book deals basically with *Mus musculus* – as well as *Rattus norvegicus* – it is prudent to take a brief look at the other varieties of mouse available on the market.

## Japanese Waltzing Mouse

This will inevitably make an appearance sometime, due to the practice among a certain number of dealers of offering it as a pet; but since its gyrations are a result of in-bred defects of the inner ear and it comes from a very weakened strain, it should never be bought by a serious breeder.

## Deer Mouse

The American Deer Mouse, despite its name, is one of the 570 species of *cricetidae* – a term that also includes hamsters and gerbils – but since it looks so very much like the House Mouse, apart from its colour, and can be reared in virtually the same manner, it is included here. *Peromyscus leucopus* is found in large numbers over most parts of North and Central America and has made a niche for itself in many types of habitat, from dense woodland to open prairie. The same size as the Fancy Mouse, its fur ranges from dark brown to a soft sandy shade, the darker tones being subdued by the sandy tips to the hairs on its sides and back; its belly and feet are white, giving rise to the more descriptive name of White Footed Deer Mouse, though it is also known as the Black-eyed Mouse and the Gopher Mouse, due to its occasional habit of living in old gopher holes. Its ears are slightly larger than those of *Mus musculus*, but its tail is the same proportionate length.

The Deer Mouse's diet in captivity differs from that of the other mice only in that it is fond of nuts; the animal can be tamed to a high degree, but since fewer generations separate it from its purely wild ancestors it can show more timidity, which can be overcome with a little more handling.

*Peromyscus* will live for four to five years in captivity, and will breed freely, especially during the summer, though perpetually warm quarters will induce breeding throughout the year.

## Dormice – *the Hazel Dormouse*

Dormice, too, belong to a different family, fitting between the *muridae*, the rats and mice, and *cricetidae*, the hamsters and deer mice. The name of this little creature stems from the French *dormeuse*, 'sleeping', aptly describing the hibernating habit shared by all ten members of the family *gliridae*.

The Hazel Dormouse has a number of aliases: by any name it is recognised as being a chubby little creature with a blunt forehead and small ears set well down on the side of the head. Its tail is short, stout, and furry, quite unlike the usual concept of a mouse tail; its body length is around $3\frac{1}{2}$in wrapped in a rich deep russet-brown fur.

The Hazel Dormouse, *Muscardinus avellanarius*, now becoming rare in the wild, is, like the Deer Mouse, prone to timidity in captivity, but can be well tamed to make a rewarding pet, though it will have the tendency to want to hibernate if it is kept in the temperate latitudes and its body rhythms allowed to fluctuate with the seasons. An animal which has shown the first signs of hibernation will need extra food and bedding material and must be allowed to sleep undisturbed until woken naturally by the increasing daylight and warmth of the spring days: to disturb the body rhythm by moving the animal into the artificial environment of a heated and lit room after it has hibernated can easily prove fatal.

If the pet is to be kept active throughout the winter, it must be housed in a room in which it cannot respond to the changing seasons — and the dormouse owner who switches off his central heating and goes for a fortnight's skiing holiday in January must expect to find his pet hibernated, or even dead, on his return.

A dormouse's diet resembles that of a rat, with a plentiful supply of apples — the animal will eat up to two a day, but one in two days is a fair ration — and its cage should also be larger than usual, since, despite its name, the animal is very active. Possibly because of its higher metabolic rate, its life span is seldom more than three years.

## Fat Dormouse
The Fat Dormouse, *Glis glis*, a native of southern Europe and the Mediterranean region, has been known since ancient times as the Edible Dormouse because the Romans considered it a delicacy and fattened it on walnuts. Much larger — 12in — 14in including its tail — the squirrel-like animal carries far more meat than other European rodents, the modern introduction of the coypu being the exception.

*Glis* was introduced into England at the turn of the century when Lord Rothschild imported some to his estate at Tring, Hertfordshire. The inevitable escapees from this stock have now populated the surrounding area; the animals live mostly in outhouses and barns, as distinct from their former woodland habitat.

*Glis*, in captivity, needs a larger box than its mouse cousins, and must be handled more carefully, since its tail is so fragile it can easily snap off.

## Yellow-necked Mouse
The Yellow-necked Mouse, *Apodemus flavicollis*, follows the

general trend in making a good if nervous pet; 4in in body length, it is slightly more robust than the Fancy Mouse with a comparatively larger head. The yellow neck and white underside make it easily distinguished. It is found in many parts of Europe, preferring wooded environment – in captivity this should be duplicated by putting peat or leaf mould on the floor of the cage and preferably an old, rotted piece of timber for the animal to investigate and perhaps nest in. The rôle of woodland forager shows itself again in the Yellow-necked Mouse's preference for a diet of seeds, including cultivated grain; only infrequently does it eat green food, and any unwanted foliage must be removed from its cage.

## Harvest Mouse
*Micromys minutus.* Apart from being one of Britain's smallest wild mammals, and the only one with a prehensile tail, it is one of the few mice which does not mark out its territorial bounds with dabs of urine – hence it makes a cleaner-smelling pet.

This lack of boundary marking in the male is explained by the animal's territory being mostly the three-dimensional world of the cornfield, especially during the natural breeding season from April to September in the northern termperate zones. With a body length of $2\frac{1}{2}$in, and a tail as long again, the chestnut-coloured back and the white throat and underbelly frequently cause it to be confused with the Yellow-necked Mouse.   In captivity *micromys* has been known to live five years, though it seldom passes its third summer; it will breed freely in captivity once it has established itself in amenable surroundings, which should include a deep peaty floor-covering and a very loose sheaf of cornstalks.

## Wood Mouse
The only other species of wild mouse that is likely to be found in captivity in the average private collection, is the handsome Long-tailed Field Mouse, *Apodemus sylvaticus*, often known as the Wood Mouse.

## Kangaroo Rat
Few species of rat, other than *Rattus norvegicus*, lend themselves to taming as pets, the occasional Kangaroo or Desert Rat, *Dipodomys desertii* being about the only contender. The Kangaroo Rat, a native of the drier grasslands and semi deserts of North and Central America, grows to 14in, with a tail an additional 8in; with tiny forepaws and very long hind legs, it is a kangaroo in miniature.

Although a creature of the desert, *dipodomys* does not like high temperatures, and in captivity thrives best between 15°C and 20°C, and for an animal of the drylands shows a healthy liking for drinking water. It lives on seeds, which in captivity may be supplemented with grain, seeding grasses, green food, and hamster mix, with an occasional mealworm as a treat. The Kangaroo Rat is a burrower in the wild, and, as a pet, needs a cage at least as large as a rabbit hutch, with sand or peatmoss, or a mixture of both, as the flooring material.

With distinct mouselike facial features, the Kangaroo Rat is usually light sandy-brown, with white flashes on its head and cheeks and around the bold, black eyes, while the belly is almost all white. Alone among the pets described in this book, it has the habit of storing food in the enlarged pockets of its cheeks.

# Choosing a pet.

Inclination will determine whether the animal one chooses is for a pet or for breeding and exhibition work. Availability of space will usually decide whether that animal is to be a mouse or a rat. In either case, the actual selection can present a problem to the inexperienced.

It is perhaps best to obtain the initial stock from a reputable breeder specialising in exhibition-class animals, since he cannot afford to use substandard strains.

As with many other rodents, rats and mice will reflect their general condition in their fur: unhealthy livestock usually having dull and uneven coats that are rough to the touch. In addition, the eyes may appear sunken and the animals generally listless; in the healthy creatures the opposite of all these indications is true: coats are shiny, eyes sparkling and bold.

Other signs of quality strains are found in bodies that are slender while still being firm, claws that are intact and free from deformities, and a perpetual state of alertness without aggression. Warning signs that are clearly evident are body sores and bald patches, lumps, sores, or kinks in the tail – which may also be without its tip – and ears that are nicked or injured.

Aggression in a pet may be suspected if the seller shows any reluctance to handle his livestock, in which case the buyer should show even more reluctance in completing the deal.

The best age at which to buy a pet is from five to six weeks when it can be more easily tamed. If contemplating more than one, without wanting to breed, the most convenient combination is two females, since the males are more prone to squabbling and – in mice – it is they alone who produce the typical musty odour in marking their territories.

The intending breeder has the choice of a couple or a trio – two females and a male – but he should restrict himself to a simple pair unless he has extra breeding boxes available: the reasoning behind this is discussed in more detail in a later chapter.

Among the problems involved in buying a pet rat or mouse, the actual purchase price is a minor consideration; in a number of instances the breeder is glad to find a home for his surplus stock; yet at the other end of the spectrum, where several people are bidding at auction for a special animal, it may fetch several pounds. Pet stores, of course, have to pay their overheads as well as make a small profit, but nowhere is there really scope for anybody to make a handsome living in raising rats and mice for the pet market.

A suitable container for bringing home the newly purchased pet is a prime essential. While in an emergency a perforated biscuit tin will do, the perfect carrying cage is a robust wooden box with a glass front: something that a do-it-yourself addict can build in a short while.

This cage should be as large as reasonably possible, certainly large enough to allow the animal to move around in comfort. The basic requirements are adequate ventilation, and a sleeping compartment one third the overall length. The fundamental rules applying to all rodent houses must also be followed: all parts of the interior must be accessible for thorough cleaning and must be free from any protruding splinters or nail points. The edges of the glass panel should be sanded smooth: an ordinary power drill with a medium-grade sanding disc will do this quite satisfactorily. But whatever box is used, it is preferable to the rather traumatic experience – for the animal – of being brought home inside a jacket pocket or up a shirt sleeve.

# Handling and housing

Rats are much more trusting than mice and respond more readily to the human voice, yet they have a greater tendency to use their teeth – which they can do to good effect.

The correct method of picking up a rat is to put the lifting hand over the animal's back, fingers towards its tail, its mouth by your wrist. Gently but firmly close the hand so the thumb tucks in by one flank and the third and little fingers tuck in by the other; lift the animal and place it on the upturned palm of the other hand, then take a firm hold of the base of the rat's tail to prevent it falling or jumping.

On no account should one lift a rat by its tail – this verges on cruelty – nor by the scruff of its neck, which is undignified and does not help in establishing a rapport with the pet. And approaching the animal from behind can have disadvantages: the slight shock to the animal can result in a nip in the fingers.

A bite from a Fancy Rat or Mouse is not poisonous, and should therefore be treated as one would a normal small cut, but if a large number of animals is being kept, with the consequent increase in the risk of being bitten, a regular tetanus injection would serve as a useful precaution.

A mouse, being so much lighter, can be picked up by the base of the tail, reached after gently caressing the head, and then the back, with one's forefinger. Holding the tail between forefinger and thumb, transfer the mouse to the upturned palm of the other hand, again retaining a hold on the tail base to avoid accidental injury by falling.

One should not try handling the animals excessively in the early days; the pet needs first to become accustomed to its owner's voice and scent before the intrusion of the comparatively large hand; the offering of tiny titbits between the fingertips is a useful way of breaking those early signs of panic.

Since the mouse has a delicate internal mechanism that quicky responds to changes in the temperature around it, the animal will become listless and almost dazed if it stays on the hand for too long, rather as a human can feel drained of all energy on a sweltering hot day. This failing can be turned to an advantage if a pet mouse loses body heat through falling into cold water or being exposed to chill draughts: it will bound back to its normal energetic self after being held for a few moments inside warm, cupped hands.

The importance of an equable temperature in the cages can

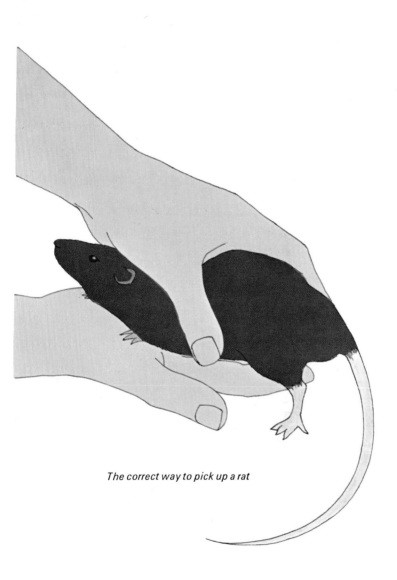

*The correct way to pick up a rat*

easily be seen. The animals' living quarters must also be kept free from damp and direct sunlight, but must be in a position where the air can circulate freely: although a colony of mice or rats will live happily in a shed or outhouse, the single pet should be kept indoors.

There are many types of commercially made cages on the market today, but since in many cases they are made to appeal to the pet owner and not to the pet, they are usually far too small. Although mice and rats are very adaptable, one should ensure that the best and largest cage is provided so that the pet will feel at home from the start.

Size is perhaps of the greatest importance, and is governed by the number of animals to be housed. A simple rule is to allow one square foot of floor space per mouse, and double this size per rat, though the larger the cage the better.

The design and size of cages can be modified to suit varying requirements: if we accept the basic norm as being 18in × 10in as the base size, with a height of 9in, to house two Fancy Mice or one rat, then the formula can be altered easily. Double the number of inhabitants and increase the volume of the cage by 50 per cent. Increase the cage height and remove half the shelf for Harvest Mice; make it larger still for the Kangaroo Rat.

Having limited the animal's movement by confining it to a cage, one must now make that cage as attractive as possible, by simulating the conditions of the wild and by giving the inhabitant something to occupy its mind and body.

The floor covering for the House Mouse can range from clean dry sawdust to cat litter, sand, peat moss or any other clean non-toxic absorbent material. It should be about 2in deep all over the floor area and should never be allowed to remain in the cage once it is damp.

Nesting material can vary widely from unprinted non-glossy paper to clean sacking, but hay is the most widely used since it also forms part of the animals' diet. Nest boxes can also be provided – though rats tend to disdain them – but since they take up valuable floor space they should be fixed either on a shelf or direct to the cage side, with suitable access.

While the main living quarters should be made of $\frac{1}{2}$in planed floorboard, chipboard, or thick ply, the nest box can be built of thinner material, its size again depending on the number of mice it is to house: a rough guide is that a box for one mouse should be large enough to hold four at a squeeze. The box should have a lift-off lid for easy observation, and the mouse entrance hole should be 1½in in diameter to allow the biggest animal to get in with ease.

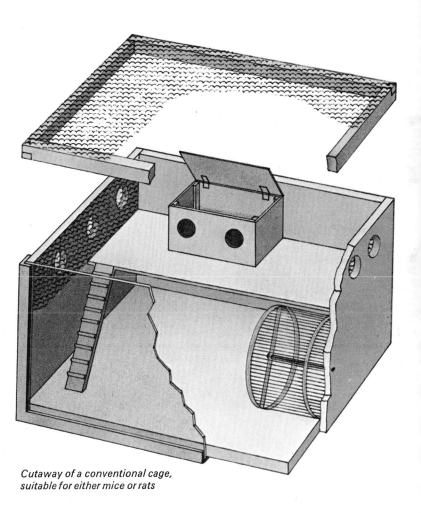

*Cutaway of a conventional cage,*
*suitable for either mice or rats*

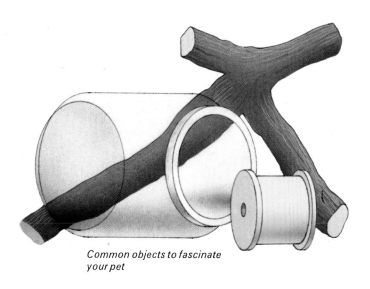

*Common objects to fascinate your pet*

Mice and rats always seem to be able to make their own fun, whether it be running in and out of their nest boxes, chasing each other, playing with nuts, or simply remaking their nests – but toys are greatly appreciated extras. Perhaps the ladder and the play-wheel are among the most popular; the latter resembling the treadmills used for human punishment in byegone ages. The only snag: make certain the spindle does not rub on the animal's back or sores and bald patches may result.

Wooden cotton reels, tree branches, rocks – all are potential playthings to the pet, but to make certain that play does not end in tragedy the toys must be without sharp edges, be unpainted, and not contain any plastic.

The idea of supplying mere playthings has a logical sequel: educational toys. Starting with simple tricks, at the end of which the rat gets his inevitable reward, one can progress to problems of reasonable complexity, which impose on the rat the need to learn, to make decisions, and to remember. Educational toys can vary from swings, seesaws, and moveable ladders to such objects as a large exercise wheel, the turning spindle of which unwinds a cord, which in turn lowers a container of food to the rat. The favourite toy of all must be the maze – starting in a small way with a few tins and

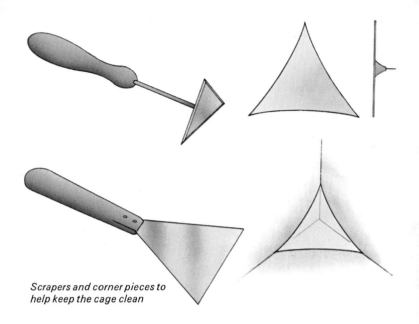

*Scrapers and corner pieces to help keep the cage clean*

boxes that have to be correctly negotiated to reach the reward, the maze can grow progressively more complex as the animal's learning abilities grow.

## Maintenance

Maintenance of the cages is relatively simple, but of extreme importance. The living quarters must be cleaned out at least once a week, more frequently if possible, especially where the unit is housing several animals. Particular care is called for in the cage corners which are a potential breeding ground for disease; these can be scraped out easily with a paint or wallpaper palette, but the better method is to block them off completely with the triangular fittings usually sold for screwing into the corners of stair treads.

Care is also called for in the daily removal of all urine-wetted flooring material: mice and rats usually reserve the same spot for this purpose so the task is somewhat simplified. Overturned water bowls can also be a source of trouble.

Other maintenance can be brought down to a twice-yearly burn or scrub-out of the cage. The scrub, with warm water and disinfectant, is probably safer than the burn-out, where there is the slight risk of charring the inside with over-use of the blowlamp.

# Feeding and nutrition

Feeding one's own pets is one thing, feeding the wild mice of the district is another. If the pets and their food supply are to be kept in a shed, the breeder must take great care to ensure that wild mice do not get access to the food. Pillage is the lesser problem, since the wild creatures may be carrying disease or parasites which the caged animals have no way of avoiding, and for which they may well have a low natural immunity.

Since a wild colony, having located a reliable source of food, will base its economy on it and breed, the importance of denying the food in the first instance is of no mean importance.

Removing the intruders, even after cutting off their sustenance, also presents problems, since one cannot use poison for fear of it reaching the caged animals – a humane mouse breeder would also shrink from inflicting such pain on other creatures. While the food-baited cage-trap is the best cure, the prevention undoubtedly lies in proper storage of the food.

Bulk quantities of dry fodder are best kept in rust-free containers fitted with suitable airtight lids; the large plastic dustbins now sold at hardware stores are ideal for the purpose, while on a smaller scale biscuit tins or lunch boxes are equally suitable.

Storage of hay can perhaps present the greatest problem, as one small bale will keep even a large mousery going for many weeks. The stock must therefore be absolutely dry, as must the plastic dustbin in which it is kept, and the quantity purchased at any time must not be excessive. An alternative to bin storage is available in the form of plastic bags, the hay having been put through a chopper.

Although feeding one's pets appears to be the lightest responsibility, since they will eat almost anything offered, there are certain very important guidelines to be observed.

Rats and mice eat basically the same food, the only difference being the quantity, but the diet must be sufficiently varied, with due attention to the proteins and vitamins that are essential to preserve a healthy stock: their properties are listed later.

One should follow a simple basic diet with the variations given as treats and titbits. A good starting diet would be based on whole-meal bread that has been allowed to go stale – *not* mouldy – and which should be soaked in cold water for about ten minutes, squeezed dry, crumbled, and have sufficient milk added to result in a tight cake-mix-like composition: dry whole oats can be

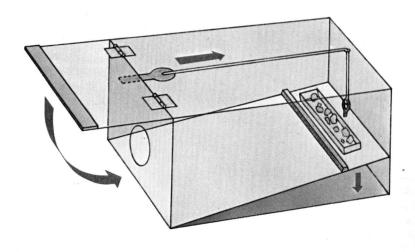

*Humane Trap: the animal activates the trap with the weight of his body*

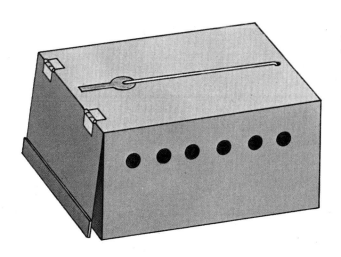

21

added to this. It is important to remember that a milk sog will eventually upset the animals' digestive systems.

Treats and titbits should take the form of any of a wide range of extras, including nibble bars (*see later*), wheat germ, millet, canary seed, hamster mix, breakfast cereal, if it is not too sweet, bread that is really hard-baked, and dog and cat biscuits : these latter succulents will give the rodents their necessary gnawing exercise. Quantities of the various ingredients will depend on the individual preference of each animal, and can be judged only by experience.

Except for the diets of specialist feeders like the Kangaroo Rat, the small rodents discussed in this book need fruit and vegetables for their moisture and vitamin content, but there is no need to make greenery a regular item on the menu ; two or three times a week is ample, to avoid stomach disorders or diarrhoea. The cultivated vegetable fare may include turnips, carrots, spinach, watercress, and the members of the *brassica* family – cabbage and Brussels sprouts – with the addition of peas, either raw or cooked. Unfortunately these foods tend to make the pets' urine somewhat smelly, and carrots lying around the cage can stain the fur, causing disaster on the show bench. Apples, pears, bananas and tomatoes present no problems and are very much appreciated.

*VITAMINS ESSENTIAL TO A HEALTHY DIET*

| Vitamin A | Cod-liver oil, milk, eggs, carrots. Essential in building disease immunity. Helps eyes to perceive light. |
|---|---|
| Vitamin B | Bran, yeast, liver. Essential to nervous system/digestion. |
| Vitamin C | Fruits, green vegetables, potatoes. Essential for good skin/fur condition. |
| Vitamin D | Cod-liver oil, milk, cheese, eggs. Helps to convert calcium and phosphorous to make bones/teeth. |
| Vitamin E | Helps to reduce risk of sterility. |

One should feed these extras in the evening, with the scraps removed in the morning to avoid the risk of mould and subsequent contamination of the dry foodstuff, which can stay in the cage.

The dry food includes the treat which I described as 'nibble bars'. The recipe for these calls for 4 oz of cornflour, an equal amount of dry wheat germ, and 8 oz of mixed corn, or hamster mix, or a combination of both, with water or milk to bind. The cornflour and wheat germ are mixed with slightly excess water or milk, after which the last ingredient is added and the whole kneaded to make a stiff dough. This should be rolled out on greaseproof paper, cut into strips, and baked until hard in a low oven. The biscuits will keep indefinitely if stored in an airtight container.

There is also a wide selection of wild plants that may be used to supplement the diet, preferably as a chopped-up mixture. One must exercise extreme care in checking that the plants are free from disease and chemical contamination from spray; they should in any event be thoroughly washed and shaken dry before being offered.

Although certain plants are poisonous to varying degrees, those in the following list are purely beneficial – indeed, a number of them have applications in herbal cures, detailed in a following chapter.

**Chickweed,** for an easily digestible tonic

**Clover,** for the nervous system

**Coltsfoot,** which eases the suffering with colds

**Comfrey,** renowned for centuries for its health-giving properties

**Cow** or **Hedge Parsley**

**Dandelion** leaves for general blood conditioning

**Dead Nettle,** for its minerals

**Dock** leaves, antiseptic, internally as well as externally

**Fresh Grasses,** for their mineral and vitamin content

**Groundsel,** also a rich source of minerals

**Plantain** and **Shepherd's Purse,** for their astringent qualities

**Sorrel, Vetch,** and **Yarrow,** for general conditioning

*If this list bears strong resemblance to a medieval herbalist's compendium, it is not merely a coincidence. Country folk in Europe still appreciate the dock's power to take away the worst of a nettle sting, and cats, strictly carnivores, very often chew on a blade of grass. Why should the mouse be any different?*

There are certain variations in the standard diet which are applicable to either rats or mice, rather than to both: rats may be offered a few hazel nuts, still in their shells, and meal worms, provided these delicacies are given no more than three at a time and not more often than three times a week. Rats also appreciate raw meat, an occasional mixture of fish food with just sufficient water to bind it, and the luxury of a block of rock salt placed in a position where it cannot be soiled.

It is also important to ensure that the rats' habit of storing food is carefully checked, and any perishable material removed.

Many breeders feel that provided the bread-and-milk mixture is given, there is no need for supplementary water, but in my opinion a drinking bowl should always be available.

Both gravity-feed water bottles and heavy open pots have their advantages – and their drawbacks. Gravity bottles are perhaps the better option, despite the greater difficulty in fixing them, since they prevent contamination of the water, but they are prone to spontaneous leaking if a piece of the nesting material is allowed to come into contact with the spout. Open pots, although extremely difficult to overturn, do allow the risk of impurities entering the water, and they consequently need to be cleaned frequently. It may be worth noting that mice drink very small amounts; rats are the more thirsty animals.

## Medicines from Wild Plants

From wild plants as food to wild plants as herbal cures is but a short and logical step. Many of the plants which rodents eat as an integral part of their natural diet have medicinal qualities. Medicinally, plants have three applications: an infusion from the leaves may be administered as a liquid tonic; the part-infused leaves themselves may be applied as a poultice; or the raw vegetable matter may be chopped finely and mixed with lard – as described later – to make an ointment.

For the tonic, one must chop the required plant very finely and bring it slowly to the boil in about half a pint of water in a closed saucepan; the amount of foliage is difficult to determine without a practical demonstration, but since the resultant liquid is a tonic, and not a refined drug, it is impossible to harm the ailing animal by giving it too strong a concentration – some of the nutrients will inevitably be destroyed in the process, and the strength of the brew will also depend on the species of herb used as well as its condition.

Once the water has boiled for two or three minutes, allow it to stand overnight in a non-metallic container and strain it in the

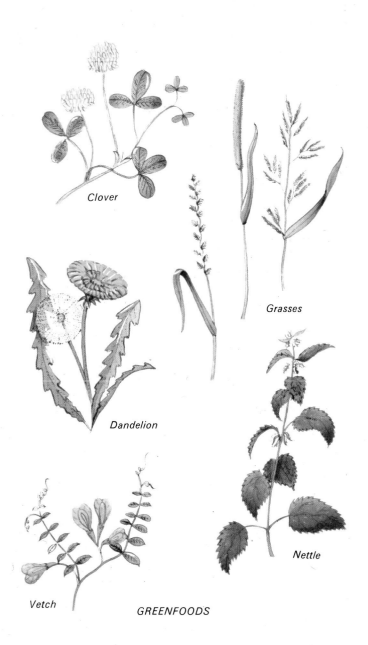

Clover

Grasses

Dandelion

Nettle

Vetch

GREENFOODS

25

morning : this is the tonic. The preparation must be stored in an air-tight, non-metallic container, out of direct sunlight, but even with these precautions it has a shelf life of no more than a week.

A poultice is made from much larger pieces of foliage dropped into water already on the boil, and allowed to cool for two or three hours ; it is then ready for use by simple application to the infected or injured area on the animal's body. If the plant is one whose leaves are not big enough to handle, the chopped fragments can be packed into an empty tea bag before steeping : indeed, for poultices that are intended to go on the animal's eye, this is the only acceptable method of application.

Between treatments – no animal will tolerate a wet leaf on its fur for very long, unless it is very ill (when a vet should already have been consulted) – the poultice can be returned to the water, but at the end of the day the preparation must be discarded : it has no shelf life at all.

Ointments for external use are a little more complex. The plant, chopped as finely as possible, is stirred into a quarter pound of pure cooking lard that has been melted in a saucepan. The mixture is simmered for at least 20 minutes, with the saucepan lid in place to avoid undue evaporation as well as to reduce the risk of fire from the molten fat.

Let the preparation cool a little before pouring it into jars where it can be allowed to set. This type of ointment can be kept for many months, but must never be used to treat injury or infection near the animal's eyes.

Knowing how to prepare the plants, we are now able to consider which to prepare and for what purposes :

**Coltsfoot** leaves and stem are particularly useful as the raw material for poultices for abscesses ; as a tonic, they can help in the recovery from colds and chills.

**Clover** – any part of the plant – makes a particularly good tonic for a successful breeding programme.

**Chickweed** is rich in minerals and its leaves and stem make a good tonic for general upsets, while a chickweed ointment is beneficial on skin or fur ailments. The tonic can also be applied on cotton-wool dabs to clean up sore eyes.

**Shepherd's purse** has already had its astringent properties praised as a straightforward food, but a tonic of the plant is also useful in cleaning cuts and grazes, while an ointment form will help in the healing

**Plantain** leaves also contain a strong healing agent and can be made into a poultice or an ointment for external use on any form of wound, particularly bites and sores ; eye infections and injuries may be treated with the poultice version only.

## INTERNAL MEDICINE DOSAGE CHART

| Animal | Dose under 13 weeks | Adult | Mother with young |
|---|---|---|---|
| Hamster/ Gerbil | $\frac{1}{4}-\frac{1}{2}$ tsp. daily | 1 tsp. daily | $1-1\frac{1}{2}$ tsp. daily |
| Rats | $\frac{1}{2}-1$ tsp. daily | 2 tsp. daily | 2–3 tsp. daily |
| Mice | Up to $\frac{1}{4}$ tsp. daily | $\frac{1}{2}-1$ tsp. daily | 1 tsp. daily |
| Rodents under 3 in. | As mice | As mice | As mice |
| Rodents under 9 in. | As rats | As rats | As rats |

*Internal medicines are best given in the animal's drinking water. If the animal refuses to drink the water, the taste can be disguised by adding the medicine to cow's milk, or, alternatively, the drinking water and medicine can be sweetened slightly with honey.*

**Dandelion** leaves and flowers make a good medicine for blood conditioning and a general pick-me-up; strong doses make a good laxative — for humans, too, as noted by the colloquial French name of the plant, *pissenlit*; 'wet the bed'.

**Groundsel** contains an antiseptic agent and is rich in minerals, particularly iron, thus making the plant ideal for a general tonic. Poultice or ointment made from the plant can be used on skin infections.

Recommended doses for adult Fancy Mice are half to one teaspoonful, with animals under thirteen weeks being given no more than a quarter teaspoonful. The dosage can be doubled for Fancy Rats, both adult and immature. The tonic may need its flavour disguised by the addition of a drop of honey or milk.

## Treatment of Common Ailments

Fancy Rats and Mice are normally hardy little animals which fare well in captivity provided the attention they receive is up to standard and their diet sufficently well balanced.

**Colds and chills** are recognised by the usual symptoms of sneezing and shivering, plus listlessness and loss of appetite. Caused by damp cages or nesting material, or by exposure to draughts, colds are incurable and have to take their course. The four to six days of suffering for the animal can be alleviated, not by any herbal cures, but by isolating the pet in a hospital cage or similarly rigged-up box, the sides of which have a slight smearing of vapour inhalant such as Vick. An ambient temperature of 18°C to 21°C and cod-liver oil on small pieces of food should help recovery.

**Pneumonia,** the next stage to colds and chills that are left untreated, begins with the same cause and produces the same symptoms. If caught early enough, the same treatment as for colds should suffice; but if the animal shows no improvement by the fifth day, the vet should be called in.

**Asthmatic attacks,** recognised by harsh breathing and constant coughing, are caused by dust in the food or the floor covering, particularly in any hay used. The treatment is to remove the animal to a dust-free environment for up to ten days, to reduce the quantity of dry foods, and also to eliminate milk from the diet, unless this is called for as a remedy for another ill.

**Diarrhoea,** easily recognised by the loose droppings and messy fur round the anal region, is caused by feeding an excess of wet foods. Give the animal dry foods only.

**Minor cuts and bites,** the result of playing or fighting, should be washed with warm water or a mild antiseptic, on a cotton bud if necessary, after which any ointment recommended for cats or hamsters – including our own shepherd's purse ointment – may be applied. Preparations specifically made for dogs should *not* be used, and injuries other than really minor ones should be referred to a vet.

**Sores,** except those caused by rubbing on playthings, usually indicate parasites under the skin or a deficiency of vitamin C. The diet can be improved by giving the animal more fruit and vegetables – remembering that excess may cause diarrhoea – while parasites are removed by dusting the animal's fur with any proprietary powder recommended for cats, and reinfection prevented by a thorough clean-out of the cage.
*Parasites in the fur itself may be assumed if the animal spends undue time in scratching, though this must not be confused with the normal meticulous grooming procedure.*

Whilst the following behaviour patterns can hardly be considered as diseases, they can be prevented by proper diet and management.

**Viciousness or shyness,** caused either by a genuine fear of the owner (who must handle his charges a little more often), or by protein deficiency, should be the sign to give by hand those extra protein titbits that were mentioned earlier.

Shyness in a breeding female, perhaps resulting in the mother killing her entire offspring, has any one of several causes: apart from a deficiency of protein, which can adversely affect the quality of her milk, there may also be a lack of vitamin B, but there is also that basic primeval fear found in all creatures of the wild, for which the only effective remedy lies in the owner buttoning up his curiosity until the litter is old enough to be shown.

Thus, apart from peace and quiet, the breeding female showing timidity needs more bran, cereal, and milk.

**Sunken eyes, listlessness, and poor appetite** are usually the hallmarks of vitamin deficiency if they are only transient; they are cured by increasing the dosage of the vitamin-rich foods, such as wheat germ or its extract, hamster tonic, green foods, goldfish food, and yeast tablets finely crushed.

The inability of a mother to produce enough milk – as opposed to producing low-quality milk – is not generally to be considered a dietary ailment. The cause is much more likely to be that the mother is too small or physically immature to bear a family, though there is also the possibility that a healthy doe has had an excessively large litter. If the young are not to die – for the mother will surely abandon them if she does not first kill them – then some or all of them must be fostered onto another female, a subject which is dealt with later. A robust mother left with one or two cubs to rear should, of course, have her diet supplemented with vitamins, and her drinking water should have some evaporated milk added.

# Breeding

Breeding is not the simple thing it would appear to be: it involves far more than putting a buck and a doe together in a cage and letting nature take its course.

With all animals in captivity, as opposed to domesticity, breeding will take place only when the environment is correct. But with mice the problem exists at both ends of the scale, for a correct setting for breeding can only too easily result in a population explosion if the brake is not applied in time.

A female can produce her first litter at six weeks of age, and can bring forth young at six-weekly intervals thereafter. The litter can be as small as one cub, or fourteen or more. If we ignore the average and select extreme conditions throughout, our initial pregnant female can give birth to 112 cubs in the year. Assuming that her offspring, the second generation, are evenly divided between male and female, and the does repeat their mother's performance, and the females of their litters do the same, then the population explosion is no figment of the imagination. If we stop the fifth and successive generations from propagating, while still allowing all others to breed for the rest of the year, we shall have a total population in excess of seven million.

If we allow the fifth generation to breed on, but stop the experiment at the end of the year when the eighth generation females have produced just one litter, we have a total population of almost thirty-four thousand million – ten times the human population of the world.

While it is inconceivable that this theoretical multiplication could ever take place, nonetheless it serves to show that fecundity is its own problem.

Thus, the basic requirement for the mouse breeder is two cages – one each for the male and the female. A third and possibly a fourth cage will be required if the offspring are not to interbreed.

For selective breeding it is far better to have a trio – one buck and two does – which will at once call for three breeding boxes: one for the male after his duty is done, and one each for the does and their families; the offspring will have to be segregated very soon, needing more cages, and one must remember that too many males together will fight.

It is, however, practicable to allow the two pregnant females to share the same nesting box – and indeed the same nest – during the confinement and birth; the mothers may help each other even to the degree of suckling each other's young. The practicability has its limits if one wishes to separate identical cubs and their identical mothers; so for many purposes in a planned breeding pogramme, the two females of a trio who are allowed to share a nest should have distinctive markings or colours.

The buck in the trio – or the buck from a pair – should be removed once there are visible signs of pregnancy in the females; with a gestation period of nineteen to twenty-one days, there is little time to spare for the necessary task of building the nest – for which, of course, extra hay should be provided.

If the birth is to take place in a specially prepared breeding box, it must be sterilised a few days before the due date, supplied with adequate material, and the drinking water supplemented with, or replaced by, milk – and the animals given sufficient time to acclimatise themselves to the new environment before they have their young, or there may be difficulties resulting in the mothers killing their offspring.

If good, healthy stock is selected, with a minimum age of twelve weeks, then one may expect a litter of about seven pink, furless, toothless, and blind cubs.

At eight to ten days the young open their eyes; around twelve days they have their teeth, although they will continue to suckle for another twelve to twenty days, or longer if allowed.

When weaned, the mother should be taken from the cubs – not the cubs from the mother – since she can stand the shock of new surroundings very much better; if space is at a premium, the female can be returned to a cage shared with other females. For her sake, as well as for the sake of the next generation, she should not be introduced to the male for at least a fortnight. The young must be sex segregated by their sixth week; while the females can be housed together, the young males will require individual accommodation by their eighth week if they are to be prevented from fighting.

The breeding of rats is a little different since family ties are much stronger; the sire can be left in the cage while the young are weaned; when the young have themselves reached maturity they still show respect for their parents and the male offspring very rarely squabble with their father.

For these reasons a pair of animals is preferable to a trio.

The gestation period of *rattus* is around twenty-one to twenty-three days, with an average seven cubs to the litter, though

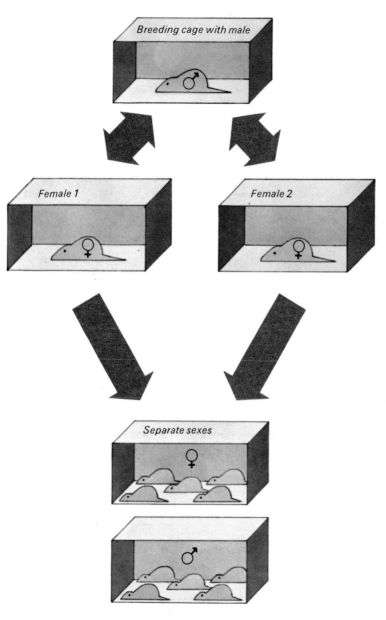

POPULATION CONTROL

sixteen is not all that rare and more have been recorded. The young develop faster than those of mice, and can be weaned at two to three weeks, just after they start to run around the cage. Puberty is reached at ten to twelve weeks, but to maintain good stocks, breeding should not be allowed under the age of sixteen weeks.

It is evident that the prudent breeder must be able to sex his animals infallibly: this is not too difficult a task since the genital organs of the male protrude as a small blob, some little distance from the anus, while the female's genital opening is much closer to the anus.

Surprisingly, it is easier to sex the animals at two to three days old, when the females of both rats and mice will show two rows of immature teats, the male organs having yet to make themselves noticed.

For the exhibition breeder, the job is not merely one of biology; in selecting various characteristics which he wishes to accentuate, he must have a proper breeding programme, which calls for a fool-proof identification system. The customary means of recognition is to identify each male by a number and each female by a letter or combination of letters. Breeding cards, with this basic identification, are kept on the outside of the animal's cage and kept up to date throughout the pet's life: to compensate for the loss of a card – marauding wild mice will readily eat them – all the information should also be recorded in a log book.

As has already been hinted, breeding involves more than merely putting male and female together: the art lies in selecting the right pair to strengthen or perpetuate the desired characteristics.

Without delving too far into the science of genetics, three basic terms can be examined:

**In-breeding**

Let us assume we are striving to perfect the hood colouration and definition which is evident on two related rats of opposite sex. If we breed from these, the chances are good that in at least two cubs – one of each sex – the hood will be a little nearer the desired result. The feature is now to be bred in to the strain, by mating these two from the same litter, and selecting the best from their offspring. By careful selection within each generation, the ultimate result will be an animal with exactly the markings and colour required – but the selection must be very carefully done, or undesirable characteristics will also be fixed in the strain. Not unnaturally it is this side-effect which has cast something of a slur on this method of breeding.

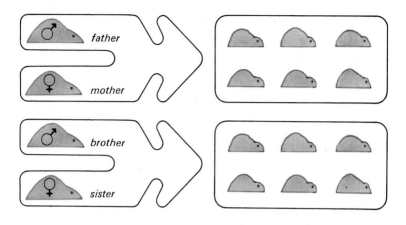

▲ *IN-BREEDING. Mate pair with inferior markings. From this litter mate superior brother and sister.*

▼ *BREEDING BACK. Mate one marked with an unmarked. From their litter mate the best marked cub with the parent.*

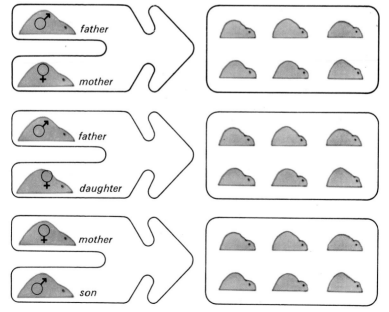

## Breeding back

Let us assume we are still faced with the same problem of how to improve a rat's hood in succeeding generations, but this time with only one such animal from which to breed. We must of necessity introduce a mate without the required marking: the quality of the hood will range from very good to very bad in the cubs from the mating. The offspring which shows the hood to the best advantage is now selected and mated with its hooded parent – and is later mated with its own selected offspring, a method which will, in time, almost eliminate the blood line of the original unhooded cross.

The basic difference now becomes apparent: the first method is selective within the same generation while the second bridges back a generation.

## Line breeding

A more detailed study of genetics will amplify what has already been suggested – that in-breeding can result in a weakening of other traits while strengthening the one for which one is selecting. Line breeding goes some way to relieve the problem.

It is obviously helpful to have two distinct strains of in-bred animals running concurrently: not only are one's chances of success doubled, but one's risks of failure are halved. At about the fifth generation of the line an out-cross can be made: a male mating not with his sister but with his cousin three times removed. This can be the beginning of another line to be in-bred, while still retaining the original two; it could also be the signal to phase out one of the strains, although by doing this one loses the later opportunity of injecting another genetic shot-in-the-arm.

A selected cub from the out-cross litter could also be bred back, and the young from that mating either bred back again or in-bred: the combinations begin to multiply.

The key, therefore, to sensible selective breeding lies not in choosing from the entire stock the buck and doe which come closest to the desired effect, then throwing their young back into the melting-pot and starting again on the same principle: this is chancing to luck. One must create continuity of the blood line at all costs, whether it is strengthened by the occasional out-cross or refined by continued in-breeding. The need for detailed and accurate record cards is at once self-evident.

So also is the need for an outlet for the mice that are not selected for breeding !

The breeder with show winners and good connections is always able to sell off his surplus stock; in many cases most of his litters are spoken for before they are born. The novice, or the breeder with poor connections, will have to rely on his friends, the local newspaper, or the nearest pet shop, none of which is likely to allow him to do more than break even on expenses.

## Fostering

When one is breeding along a selected blood line there is little one can do to prevent the accidental loss of an animal — assuming that housing and diet are maintained at the highest standard — but there is a remedy to that annoying problem of finding a doe which cannot or will not rear its young. Whilst a repetition of this trait is a sign that it must at all costs be bred out, a single instance can be overcome by fostering the young onto a mother which has a conveniently-sized litter of the same age.

Since the need to foster can arise for a number of reasons — inability to lactate; too large a litter; nervousness — if one is well advanced on a particularly valuable bloodline, a very useful insurance is to have several females mated at the same time so that the cubs with the desired traits can immediately be transferred to a more receptive female if their natural mother is unable to bear the burden.

A rudimentary precaution necessary before introducing foster cubs is to impregnate them with the odour of their new guardian, or they may be considered as intruders and killed. The easiest way of doing this is to roll the cubs very carefully in some floor covering, preferably slightly moistened from the foster mother's urine, and introduce them to their new nest while the female is temporarily removed.

At this point the advantages of trio breeding with mice are at once apparent: since females sharing the same nesting box readily play with and suckle each other's cubs, a foster mother is immediately on hand if needed. The only requirement is that the two females must be of distinctive colouring.

That Fancy Rats breed better in pairs than in trios is no real disadvantage, since the female rat is less likely to need her offspring fostered; she can always produce enough milk for her litter, no matter how large it may be.

# Exhibiting

Sooner or later the urge will come to show one's stock. To stand some chance of success – indeed, to get the animals on the judging bench – requires a basic instruction in the preparation and presentation of Fancy Rats and Mice.

The beginner will almost certainly find that a local club show is his best breaking-in ground for the larger and more competitive world of the agricultural exhibition or county show, but the small club must not be considered as an opportunity for light-hearted experimenting since the competition, if not the field, is just as keen; indeed, some of the greatest awards can be won at this type of show.

The competition is normally reserved for standard animals – those which conform to the basic colour or marking requirements listed on succeeding pages – but pet shows as such are far from scarce, either being held separately or in conjunction with a standard show. Pets are judged only on their tameness and their condition, but the exhibitor of a standard animal will have a number of criteria to meet.

Preparation and presentation really go hand-in-hand, since slackness in one will ruin all the work in the other. The first essential, therefore, is a sufficient range of cages: one for bringing the pet to the show, if the distance involved is such to allow the animal to foul part of its bedding; another cage for grooming prior to the show's opening; and the third, the actual exhibition cage.

Travelling cages are discussed elsewhere; grooming cages are simple, merely being a box or a well-ventilated biscuit tin with a good lining of hay and sawdust in which the animal can burrow, thus cleaning and drying its fur.

While the animal kept merely as a pet may be displayed in almost any type of gnaw-proof container – obviously, appearances even here will have some subconscious influence on the judge – the standard rat or mouse bred for exhibition must be shown in a proper pen, the type almost universally adopted being the Maxey cage, named after the founder of the mouse fancy.

The late Walter Maxey devised a metal container which fulfilled the basic needs of a show cage: easily carried; easily cleaned; easily fastened; easily opened. While the first three qualities are obvious requirements, it can so often be overlooked that the judge must take the animal out of its cage and hold it, and a mass of twisted wire and padlocks will eliminate the animal from the contest.

## ENTRY FORM

NAME: John Smith    CLUB:

ADDRESS: 14 High St,
ANYTOWN.

| CLASS | OFFICIAL USE | ALSO IN CLASSES | DATE OF BIRTH | REMARKS |
|---|---|---|---|---|
| 26 | | 31, 40, 45. | 1/8 | Dutch Ad. buck mouse |
| 49 | | 53 | | Hooded Ad rat |
| | | | | Total: 2 mice 1 rat |
| | | | | 6 classes @ Total enclosed £ |

With the emphasis on prevention rather than cure, the animal – having been pre-groomed at home – should have nothing but dry food in its travelling cage ; moisture can be provided in the form of a slice of raw potato. Animals with white fur are particularly liable to develop noticeable stains from the wrong sort of food being offered them during the journey, carrot being notorious for discolouring the fur the moment the two come into contact. The pre-grooming involves removing all such stains by damping the dirtied area and rubbing a trace of cornflour into it, brushing out when dry. This may need to be done several times, thus the best precaution of all is to concentrate on a basically dry diet several days before the show is due.

A number of clubs allow the powdering of white animals as a normal grooming process, but whether or not your club agrees with the practice, it is important that no trace of cornflour be visible during the actual judging.

Grooming at the show itself should be reduced to a minimum, the romp in the hay of the grooming box being perhaps the major preparation, allowing the animal to do most of the work itself. The last preparation before transferring the animal to its show cage, is the one which can so often lose – or gain – those vital points that are necessary for victory : putting the glossy sheen on the coat. This can be achieved by careful grooming with the same sort of soft brush that is used on cats prior to shows, followed by gently stroking the fur with a silk cloth until the sheen really glows.

The showcage itself must not carry any possible clues to the identity of the owner – another reason for adopting a uniform style of cage – and for this reason the only labelling allowed is a simple printed stick-on tag bearing details of the show class and a code number by which the show manager alone can identify the owner. Any other marking that could be construed as a pre-arranged sign to the judge will disqualify the animal.

After all these preparations and precautions, the rest is up to the animal !

### Didn't win ?

Few novices do gain awards at their first attempt, for exhibiting rats and mice is no exception to the general rule of learning by trial and error. During the show, the keen beginner can learn a great deal by sizing up the opposition, but the best advice is undoubtedly obtained by asking the judge direct – *after* the show – exactly why he faulted a certain animal and how the defects can be made good

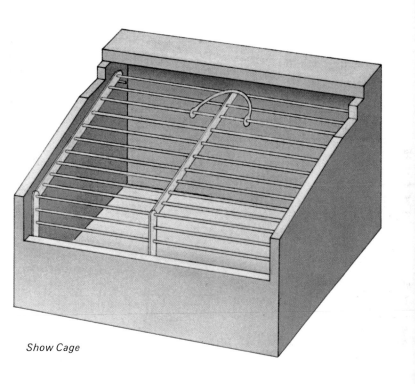

*Show Cage*

next time. Judges, after all, have risen from the ranks of the exhibitors and are usually keen to impart any information which will result in the advancement of the hobby : a disgruntled exhibitor is one who can so very easily quit the show benches forever, leaving the judge in an unenviable position.

Prizes themselves vary from the simple card and rosette to a money award or another kind of trophy, but it is not the prize itself which is the end result – the reward comes in the winning of it, an indication that one is heading in the right direction.

## Show schedules

Undoubtedly the most confusing part of the whole exhibition game is the vast number of abbreviations that occur, a necessity if the schedule is to appear in the advertising columns of the specialist magazines. Set out below is an extract from a typical schedule, with the abbreviations explained.

| CLASS No. | SELFS | | |
|---|---|---|---|
| 10 | P.E.W. Ad. | 35 | Chin. and fox u/8 |
| 11 | P.E.W. u/8 | 36 | A.O.V. Ad. |
| 12 | Blk/choc. Ad. | 37 | A.O.V. u/8 |
| 13 | Blk/choc. u/8 | 38 | A.O.V. Chall. Ad. (D) |
| 14 | A.O.C. Ad. | 39 | A.O.V. Chall. u/8 (d) |
| 15 | A.O.C. u/8 | | |
| 16 | S. Chall. Ad. (D) | | **DUPLICATED CLASSES** |
| 17 | S. Chall. u/8 (d) | 40 | Stud buck. |
| | | 41 | Brood doe. |
| | **TANS** | 42 | Juvenile. |
| 18 | Cham. Ad. | 43 | Novice. |
| 19 | Cham. u/8 | 44 | Supporters. |
| 20 | Silver Ad. | 45 | G.C. Ad. |
| | | 46 | G.C. u/8 |
| 25 | Tan Chall. u/8 (D) | | |
| | | | **RAT CLASSES** |
| | **MARKED** | 47 | White Ad. |
| | | 48 | White u/13 |
| 26 | Dutch Ad. | 49 | Hooded Ad. |
| 27 | Dutch u/8 | 50 | Hooded u/13 |
| 28 | A.O. Mrk. Ad. | | |
| 29 | A.O. Mrk. u/8 | | **PET CLASSES** |
| 30 | Mrk. Chall. Ad. (d) | 55 | Pet mouse white. |
| 31 | Mrk. Chall. u/8 (D) | 56 | Pet mouse A.O.C. |
| | | 57 | Pet rat white. |
| | **A.O.V.** | 58 | Pet rat A.O.C. |
| 32 | Agouti Cinn. Ad. | 59 | Pet mouse G.C. |
| | | 60 | Pet rat G.C. |

## Abbreviations explained

| | |
|---|---|
| A.A. | Any age |
| Ad. | Adult – mice over eight weeks, rats over thirteen weeks |
| A.O.C. | Any other colour |
| A.O.V. | Any other variety |
| A.V. | Any variety |
| B.E. | Black eyed |
| B.E.W. | Black-eyed white |
| B.I.S. | Award for Best in Show |
| Blk. | Black |
| B.O.S. | Best opposite sex |
| C. | Commended, i.e. awarded 7th place |
| C.C. | Championship certificate |
| Cham. | Champagne coloured |
| Chin. | Chinchilla |
| Choc. | Chocolate coloured |
| Chall. | Challenge |
| Cinn. | Cinnamon coloured |
| (D) or (d) | Duplicated – the animal must be entered in two classes |
| | according to the rules of the exhibition |
| G.C. | Grand Challenge |
| H.C. | Highly commended, i.e. awarded 6th place |
| L/H | Long haired |
| Mrk. | Marked |
| P.E. | Pink eyed |
| P.E.W. | Pink-eyed white |
| R. | Reserve, i.e. awarded 4th place |
| S. | Self coloured |
| T. | Tan coloured |
| Tri. | Tricoloured |
| u/8 | Under eight weeks old, applied to mice |
| u/13 | Under thirteen weeks old, applied to rats |
| Uns. | Under-standardised |
| V.H.C. | Very highly commended, i.e. awarded 5th place |
| Wht. | White. |

# Show standards

A mouse for exhibition standard must fit certain broad qualifications laid down by the National Mouse Club, from whose *Rule and Standards Book* the following information is reproduced.

The animal must be long in the body with a long, clean head not detracted by a too fine or a too pointed nose; the eyes should be large, bold, and prominent, and the large tulip-shaped ears, free from creases, should be carried erect with plenty of width between them. The back should be slightly arched over the loin and have a racy appearance, leading to a tail which should stand out well, with a thick base, gradually tapering like a whip to a fine tip, and without the least kink. The tail should approximately equal the body in length.

The mouse's demeanour should also be perfectly tractable and free from any tendency towards undesirable habits, fits, or similar behavioural ailments.

A penalty of 20 points is incurred for any animal with sunken eyes, kinked tail, or a proven tendency to fits; an animal without whiskers is automatically disqualified.

### Colour varieties of Fancy Mice and Rats

There are so many varieties that space permits the mention of only a very select few; many, though, are crossbreeds and therefore the set list of recognised colours issued by the NMC is also selective.

The colours have been grouped into four sections for easy classification. They are:

### Group One – Selfs

The name 'self' is given to an animal of only one colour, which must be consistent everywhere on the body. The recognised self colours are:

Black, eyed black

Black, eyed white

Blue (slate blue) eyed black

Chocolate, eyed black

Red (deep rich auburn), eyed black

Fawn, eyed pink

Dove (dove grey), eyed pink

Cream, eyed pink

Cream, eyed black

Champagne (pale pink), eyed pink

Pink, eyed white

Silver, eyed pink

Silver, eyed black

*Black Mouse*

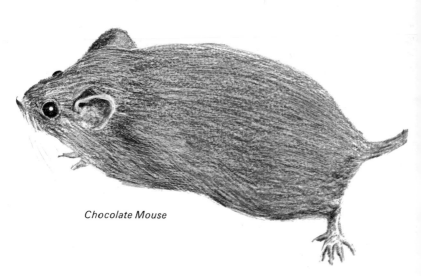

*Chocolate Mouse*

*Blue Mouse*

### Group Two – Tans
Tans have one distinct colour on the upper body, with the underside a clear tan, separated by a straight demarcation line. The group consists of the self colours plus tan, i.e. Black and tan, Champagne and tan.

### Group Three – Marked
This group consists of white animals with some additional coloured markings on the body. The varieties recognised are:

| | |
|---|---|
| Broken | Dutch |
| Even | Himalayan |
| Rump White | Tricoloured |
| Variegated | |

### Group Four – A.O.V.
Any Other Variety, as the group is called, embraces many colours and combinations not included in the other three groups and includes the more unusual breeds, such as the Agouti, the Seal Point Siamese, the Long Haired, Satin Coated, and Astrex. A few of the breeds within the group are:

| | |
|---|---|
| Agouti | Seal Point |
| Argente | Sable |
| Astrex | Pearl |
| Marten Sable | Cinnamon |
| Chinchilla | |

## Exhibiting mice

The points list issued by the National Mouse Club in its *Rule and Standards Book* for all standard varieties of mouse specifies the first 35 points thus:

| | |
|---|---|
| Body shape and carriage | 10 points |
| Size | 5 |
| Ears | 5 |
| Eyes | 5 |
| Muzzle | 5 |
| Tail | 5 |
| total | 35 points |

to which are added 65 points awarded for specific characteristics of the various varieties, thus:

## Self Varieties

| | |
|---|---|
| Condition | 15 points |
| Colour | 50 |

*Red Mouse*

*Fawn Mouse*

*Dove Mouse*

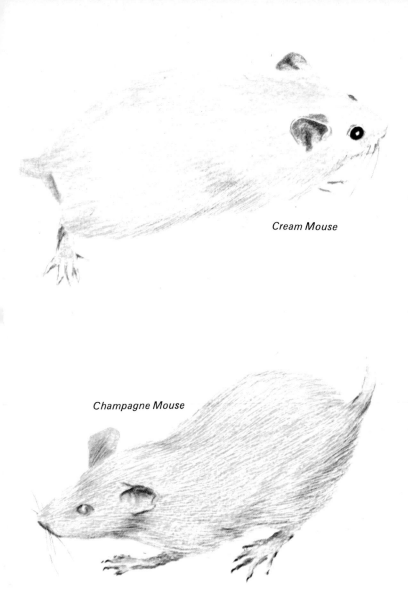

*Cream Mouse*

*Champagne Mouse*

## Tan Varieties

| | |
|---|---|
| Condition | 15 points |
| Feet | 10 |
| Tan | 20 |
| Top colour | 20 |

## Marked Varieties viz:

**Dutch,** with pink or black eyes and of any standard colour.

| | |
|---|---|
| Cheek markings, blaze, and colour | 20 points |
| Saddle | 15 |
| Undercut | 15 |
| Stops | 5 |
| Condition | 10 |

**Even,** with pink or black eyes and of any standard colour.

| | |
|---|---|
| Clearness of markings, position and colour | 55 points |
| Condition | 10 |

**Broken,** with pink or black eyes and of any standard colour.

| | |
|---|---|
| Clearness, number, position, and colour of patches | 45 points |
| Condition | 10 |
| Nose spot or patch | 10 |

**Variegated,** with pink or black eyes and of any standard colour.

| | |
|---|---|
| Uniformity of variegation and colour | 50 points |
| Condition | 15 |

**Himalayan,** with black or red eye markings as in the Himalayan Rabbit and of any standard body colour, though with as much white as possible.

| | |
|---|---|
| Nose markings | 10 points |
| Foot markings | 10 |
| Ear markings | 10 |
| Tail markings | 10 |
| Purity of body colour | 10 |
| Condition | 15 |

*Marked Mice*

**Rump White,** of any standard colour but with a white rump.

| | |
|---|---|
| Colour | 10 points |
| Rump | 10 |
| Demarcation lines | 20 |
| Feet | 10 |
| Condition | 15 |

## Any Other Varieties, viz:

**Agouti,** with black eyes, rich golden-brown top fur evenly ticked with black; belly fur golden-brown with ticking.

| | |
|---|---|
| Colour | 35 points |
| Evenness of ticking | 15 |
| Condition | 15 |

**Silver Agouti,** with black eyes, bright silver-grey fur above, evenly ticked with black; silver-grey belly without prominent ticking.
   Points as for Agouti.

**Cinnamon,** a rich golden tan all over with ticking clearly defined.
   Points as for Agouti.

**Sable,** with black eyes and a rich dark-brown top fur shading to a rich golden tan on the belly.

| | |
|---|---|
| Colour | 35 points |
| Level shading | 15 |
| Condition | 15 |

**Marten Sable,** with a rich dark-sepia top fur paling at the flanks and blending gradually to a white belly fur.

| | |
|---|---|
| Colour | 30 points |
| Level shading | 10 |
| Belly | 10 |
| Condition | 15 |

**Pearl,** which has black eyes and a very pale silver top fur tipped with grey or black, fading to a ticked whitish under the belly.

| | |
|---|---|
| Colour | 30 points |
| Evenness of tipping | 20 |
| Condition | 15 |

*Long-hair Mouse*

*Rex Mouse*

**Silver Fox,** a black-eyed breed that is distinguished by its black, blue, and chocolate top colour with white underside; the feet, flanks, and rump are ticked evenly in white.

| | |
|---|---|
| Colour | 20 points |
| Belly | 15 |
| Ticking and feet | 15 |
| Condition | 15 |

**Long Hair,** of any recognised colour but with long, dense, and silky fur.

| | |
|---|---|
| Coat | 35 points |
| Colour | 20 |
| Condition | 10 |

## Exhibiting Rats

Among the many standards for Fancy Rats are:

**Irish Black,** as self black but with an equilateral triangle on its chest and with four white feet.

| | |
|---|---|
| Colour | 35 points |
| Condition | 15 |
| Triangle | 10 |
| Shape and carriage | 10 |
| Size | 5 |
| Feet | 5 |
| Ears | 5 |
| Eyes | 5 |
| Head | 5 |
| Tail | 5 |

*Irish Black Rat*

*Hooded Japanese Rat*

**Japanese Hooded Rat,** with sides, legs, and feet a pure white and with head and saddle of any distinct colour. The hood must cover the head, throat, chin, and shoulders without a break, and the saddle should extend in a straight unbroken line down the back to the tail which must be partly coloured. The eyes can be black or ruby.

| | |
|---|---|
| Colour | 25 points |
| Head and saddle | 25 |
| Condition | 15 |
| Shape and carriage | 10 |
| Size | 5 |
| Head | 5 |
| Ears | 5 |
| Eyes | 5 |
| Tail | 5 |

**Brown Agouti,** head and top colour of which is rich ruddy brown, evenly ticked; the black belly is devoid of ticking. Black eyes.

| | |
|---|---|
| Top colour | 20 points |
| Belly colour | 15 |
| Condition | 15 |
| Shape and carriage | 10 |
| Size | 5 |
| Head | 5 |
| Eyes | 5 |
| Ears | 5 |
| Tail | 5 |
| Ticking | 15 |

**Fawn Agouti,** a light fawn evenly ticked with dark brown; the belly fur as the top but without ticking. Eyes a dark red.

Points as for Brown Agouti.

*Brown Agouti Rat*

**The Capped Rat,** which is basically the same as the Hooded Rat except for the absence of a saddle.

| | |
|---|---|
| Colour | 25 points |
| Cap | 15 |
| Blaze | 10 |
| Condition | 15 |
| Shape and carriage | 10 |
| Size | 5 |
| Head | 5 |
| Ears | 5 |
| Eyes | 5 |
| Tail | 5 |

*Capped Rat*

## Appendix
The National Mouse Club

The club, founded in 1895 with the aim of encouraging the breeding and exhibition of Fancy Mice, now embraces Fancy Rats and allied pets as well, and advises on all matters of the hobby, from the first purchase to the last showing.

The club also arranges exhibitions ranging from novitiate shows upwards, and has a large collection of trophies which are awarded at the many shows staged by the club or held under its patronage. There are also many local rodent societies in Britain and abroad, most of which are affiliated to the N.M.C.

Since secretaries change from one year to another, the author will be pleased to act as intermediary and forward to the current secretary any enquiries regarding rules, standards, subscriptions, or general advice, on receipt of a plain stamped envelope (for forwarding) and a stamped, self-addressed envelope (for reply). Enquiries from abroad should have the relevant international reply coupons.

The address is:
K. W. Smith,
10 Russell Street
LUTON
Bedfordshire
England

# Index

Distributors for
Bartholomew Pet Books

## Australia

Book Trade : Tudor Distributors Pty. Limited, 14 Mars Road,
Lane Cove 2066, New South Wales, Australia

## Canada

Pet Trade :   Burgham Sales Ltd., 558 McNicoll Avenue,
Willowdale (Toronto), Ontario, Canada M2H 2E1
Book Trade : Clarke Irwin and Company, Limited,
791 St. Clair Avenue W., Toronto, Canada M6C 1B8

## New Zealand

Pet Trade :   Masterpet Products Limited,
7 Kaiwharawhara Road, Wellington, New Zealand
Book Trade : Whitcoulls Limited, Trade Department, Private Bag,
Auckland, Wellington, or Christchurch, New Zealand

## South Africa

Book Trade : McGraw-Hill Book Company (S.A.) (Pty.) Limited,
P.O. Box 23423, Joubert Park, Johannesburg,
South Africa

## U.S.A.

Pet Trade :   Pet Supply Imports Inc., P.O. Box 497, Chicago,
Illinois, U.S.A.
Book Trade : The Two Continents Publishing Group Limited,
30 East 42nd Street, New York, N.Y. 10017, U.S.A.